TRANSFORMATION
Life to Death / Death to Life

Make Me as Beautiful as a Butterfly
Revive My Soul
Change My Colors
Bring Me Out
Lord, Have Mercy on Me

Lytoni S. Brown

Copyright © by Lytoni Brown
In 2002, 2004

All rights reserved. Printed in the United States of America. No part of this book may be used or reproduced in any manner whatsoever without permission of the author.

ISBN: 0-9771358-0-2

For more information:
Transformation04_15@hotmail.com

Photography by E. D. I. Photo

This book is dedicated:

*I want to thank to God almighty the head of my life.
I want to thank you for giving me the transformation in my life
to help me become a better person.
Without you there will be no me.
Lord I thank you and I love you.*

TRANSFORMATION
Life to Death / Death to Life

Life
Who am I

1. Agape love
2. My dream
3. My name is Eve
4. What is black
5. Old times
6. Spoken words

Death
Broken heart

7. It's Only a Dream
8. Art
9. Turning her out
10. Games
11. You said you love me.
12. One moment that's all it takes
13. Occupying my time
14. The word love loves no one

Death
Confusion

15. Unknown
16. Cold world alone
17. Life
18. Mankind
19. Pain

Life
Transformation

20. My soul was fed
21. Change my colors
22. I know
23. There is another path I can take
24. Living right

Life
Who am I

*Then the Lord God formed man of dust from
the ground, and breathed into his nostrils
the breath of life; and man became a living being
Genesis 2:7-NASB*

Agape love

Man has hit me in my face
Torn my clothes into pieces
Ridiculed me, did every thing but love me
But I walk in Agape love
With the one from above
When I pray and leave the day
I put it in God's hands
And I know everything will be ok

But Lord, at times, I find it hard
To walk in Agape Love
To
Forgive and forget
To
Love fellow men
And to treat my enemies as friends

Lord at times I find it hard
To have fellowship with hypocrites
And I wonder how all those lies
Can come from their lips
As I give them a made up hug
I pray I will never be like them

While I am in their false embrace
I see God's face
So I can't erase

The agape love within me he has placed

Agape Love that is what I want
To show
Practice
And know

If I walk in Agape Love
Until my life is done
With the one from above
Then I know victory
I will have won

My dream

My dream is to be happy
I want to live free
I don't know what the future
Has in store for me
But whatever is meant to be
I know I will rise in the sky
And be as bright as I can be
Never will I rot like spoiled milk
I will be as sweet as a strawberry
I will explode like a wild fire
So I can't be beaten
Because my knowledge
Will not be weakened
Plus my faith is too strong
To God I will hold on
all people will see
When I run I fly
I pass all the hater's by
I will not give up the race and die
I will keep on
Until
I get to the finish line

My name is Eve

My name is Eve
Came from my husband
Cause I am the mother
Of all living things
I am the coca cola shaped body
Little tits
Nice hips
Conniving chick

My name is Eve
Came after I ate
from the good and evil tree
I was deceived by Satan he taught me some
Good love making
He showed me that I hold power over a man
That lies in between my legs
That is why I act all boogie
With my nose in the air
Because I hold the weapon in between my legs

As I was using my weapon
I was deterring my soul
As I was putting my children to rest
For I am the cause of their death
I supposed to be the mother of birth
But my children are dying
They went from living for eternity
To nine hundred
To ninety-nine

Now they are dying at twenty five
And my weapon is the reason why
My children are dying
They are losing their mind
Some are walking around dead alive

Adam got tired of trying
Nothing is the truth
Now we both are lying
Deceiving the creator's plan
Seeming Adam can't trust a woman
He turn to man
But he can't stay away
So he comes back and infests my body with
AIDS
And my weapon is the reason why
Adam looks for love in every way
Form
And shape
Our daughter he rapes
She looks to release the pain
So she sex every man she date
Following her mother's sinful mistakes

My son don't have much to look up to
Because his father is less than a man
And he don't want to follow the trend
So he is in love by the fast money making
He let go of his pain in dope
His life is burning like fire on a rope
When he is thirty-five

He will have nothing to show
Because of my sins my sons
Are dying young and broke

Satan keeps lying
I am conniving
Deceiving
To get what I want and need
Adam was not created for me
Knowing I hold power in between my legs
Ignoring the tears my children shed
Forgetting about the knowledge in my mind

Because it is easier to open my legs
Refusing to feed my brain
So I keep on having children I can't raise
Aborting them everyday
In the clinic
And in other ways
Neglect my children's needs
How selfish of me

My sins is a chain reaction
At the end I get no satisfaction
Satan's laughing and relaxing
But I won't let his lies overpower me
Because of Calvary
I have the power to change
And make tomorrow a brand new day
For my name is Eve
And I am the mother of all living

What is black

What is black
According to Webster
Black is without light, evil, wicked; angry, dirty;
A person of any dark skin
A Negro

What is black?
Clever in the mind
Smart and divine
Creative with their hands
Both black men and women
As bright as a light
Won't give up unless there is a fight

What is black?
The shoes we put on our feet
The electric lamp we use to see
The ice cream we might enjoy to eat
The locks on out doors that needs a key

So Mr. Webster, next time stand corrected

Or maybe back in the day
When the book was made
Black meant negative anyways
From where the word came
Is not to be contained
The word black has been portrayed
In such a backwards way

Now the word black has formed a powerful sound
And did a total rebound
As dark as they say this word is to be
Black is brighter than what our eyes can see
Most importantly
Black is our history

So why do our society
Judge us by the color
That appears on our faces
They say we are equal
But are we really racist?

Look at you and me
Then tell me the difference that you see
If you don't look within
And you say we are different
Because the color of my skin
Then
When is being equal
Really going to begin

Old times

I am the mother
You are the father
My baby doll name is Heather
House is the game we will play
When there is cold weather

Uga uga
Black buga
Uga uga out
You hide I find
Hide and seek
I see you behind that tree
Tag you're it don't have a hissy fit
Freeze tag
Brought out some laughs

Marco polo
Marco polo
On a hot sunny day
In the pool getting cool
Marco polo
Marco polo
With my eyes closed
Hoping no one splashed me in the face
After that game
We would jump in and race

On your mark get set go

Down the street at full speed
On our bikes
In broad daylight
I hit a speed bump
And fell straight on my butt
I will go in the house and cry
My mother's special touch
Made all my tears dry up

When I look back at old times
All good times come to mind
I smile and laugh
Also shed some tears
Because my childhood
Has disappeared

Spoken words

Often my brain goes
I seem to dig inside my soul
And let my poetry flow
Most don't understand
The language that I speak
Because their knowledge is weak
I will not say many words
For my actions will show
Through spoken word
My story should be told

Death

Broken Heart

He heals the broken hearts and binds up their wounds
Psalms 147:3- NI

It's only a dream

When I first saw your face
My bones froze
The blood that flows
Through my veins
Like a river bay
Stopped instantly

When you smiled I got this sensation
Then we became God's greatest creation
I am your queen
You are my king
And together we are each other
Water on this earth full of hell
I wonder if there
Is a different way for me to feel

I look deeper than your brown skin
And when I look into your eyes
I see a real man
Now we are lovers
And more than friends

I don't care if I'm wrong
For feeling so strong
I can't deny
What my soul feels inside
Off my heart I release my protection
So I can take in all your affection

Intoxicated with your love
Breathing in internal feelings
Waking up
Dreaming

Art

No one understands the picture
But the creator
How can something be so ugly
But so beautiful
And admired by so many

How can two people
Who are misinterpreted
Find light in each other
Knowing they will never be lovers
But build a foundation
In a world that's very dark
Our friendship is just like art

Death: Broken Heart

Turning her out

Innocent
Pure as snow
For she doesn't know
He shows her so many things
Sexually
He's twenty-two
She's sixteen
She thinks it's cool
To date an older man
He takes her from a child to a woman
She tells lies
And thinks of reasons why
And how to get to him
And feel that feeling
She never felt
The hugging
The kissing
The touching
The rubbing
The licking
He's working
His way to sticking
This young innocent child
Turning her out
Teaching her how to run wild

He says "Shh" it's not going to hurt
She doesn't know from this point
Her life will be corrupt

From his aftermath
He makes her leave fast
So he can freshen up
For his next piece of young ass
She leaves with dreams knowing they would last
She goes home and calls him

But he does not return her calls
Because in his world she doesn't exist at all

Six weeks later
She lays on the doctor table
She tells him
She's contacted an STD
He says what does that
Have to do with me
She says I thought you
LOVE me
He says baby
Let's be realistic
You think I love you
You are just another
statistic

Games

You said you love me
But after you got what you wanted
It seemed like all that love faded away

I wish I could say
It took me a long time to see
You just was making a fool out of me

I admit
I was stupid
I wasn't blind
I knew what you were doing
And the game you were pulling

I thought it will be easy
To get over you

I was lying to myself
Trying to make us work

My feelings
You took as a joke

Trying to be hard
Like I am over you
Everybody knew that wasn't true

Acting innocent
Like I have no clue

Stubborn because
I was in love with you

You said you love me

You said you love me
Why did you leave me?
Love would not do half
The things you did

I thought you was different
I thought you was
true

At the end I was crying the blues
Playing the fool
Being used
By you

I gave you the key to my heart
 Knowing we weren't going to part
I thought my life revolved around you
Not knowing my life was better off
without you

I got on my knees and prayed
I asked the lord to prepare
Me for this day

The day came when
You said you did not want to stay
My eyes began to cry
I lost my mind
It seemed like my body

Shut down and
Died

Death: Broken Heart

One moment that's all it takes

One moment to laugh
One moment to cry
One moment to live
One moment to die
One moment of passion
Can lead to a lifetime of pain
One moment that's all it takes

One moment of affection
Can lead to a deadly infection
Because there was no protection
Then you wonder how can this be
Innocent when you said this can't happen to me

One moment for the gun to go bang
Now you are trying to persuade the grand jury
To see things your way
Can't any other take that mother's child's place
Now when you open your eyes
At the sunrise
You see one moment
Got you in the penitentiary

One moment for families
To be destroyed and broken
Because actions and words has been spoken
You did the math and divided
Now you realized
Without your family
you can't survive

We wish we could go back in time
Now there's nothing left to do but cry
It might have been a mistake
But one moment that's all it takes

Occupying my time

I
Occupied my time
Helping you achieve Forty Acres and a Mule
But when you got on top
you left
Putting me down
Now you are nowhere to be found

I guess
You needed a back to walk on
And a cat to split
Thru the struggle
But now the struggle is over
So why did you leave
Causing me to struggle
With a newborn child
I thought we was supposed
to struggle together
In love forever
But I guess
Love goes away
When the struggle is over

I
Occupied my time
Helping you achieve Forty Acres and a Mule
Drifting away from me
Wanting success for two
Living for three
Dreaming for three
Making long term moves for two
Forgetting about me
But when
One is gone out of three
That makes two
Leaving me to support two

Death: Broken Heart

But how can I support two
If I don't start with me
With my successes
But how can I be successful
If I am
Occupying my time
Helping you achieve Forty Acres and a Mule

I
Occupied my time
Helping you achieve Forty Acres and a Mule
When you had nothing but dust
I gave you a bed to lay on
I told you to lay your head on my heart
And listen to how much I want for you
How I was going to help you achieve your
Forty Acres and a Mule

I
Occupied my time
Helping you achieve Forty Acres and a Mule
Stepping back from being an independent woman
Cause I did not want you to feel less than a man

So I made a comfort zone
And I got so comfortable
Being one with you
Helping you
Loving you
Falling for you
Losing for you
Where were you
When I needed you
When I failed
When I struggled
When I struggled helping you
Achieve Forty Acres and a Mule

I live and learn
Not to let half the rent walk out the front door
This struggle will be
No more
Because I will make sure
I occupy my time
Helping
ME
achieve my Forty Acres and a Mule

Death: Broken Heart

The word love loves no one

My heart is crying tears
Because it is in so much fear
Fear that it might get broken again
Again I'm falling in love
What should I do
The difference is this time it's with you

Why do I have this sensation
All this crazy temptation
I pray for this feeling to go away
But hope at the same time
It will stay

In the war of love my soul has been defeated
My heart has been beaten
I'm trying to recover
And slowly building a new reconstruction
This time better my mind will function

Maybe
It's not you
Maybe it's the word love
That I love so dearly
But I have to remember
That the word has
No eyes
Nor has it a mind
The word has no heart
Nor a soul

The word shows no remorse
The word love loves no one

Death

Confusion

For God is not a God of confusion but of peace as in all the churches of the saints
1 Corinthians 14:33- NASB

Unknown

How can I summarize my story
If I have no plot?
How can I draw my conclusion
If I have no experiment?

How can I grow the branches on my tree
If I have no seed?
How can I build myself
If I have no foundation?

How can I be successful
If I have no knowledge?
How can I live luxuriously
If I have no money?

How can I love
If I have no heart?
How can I live
If I have no soul?

How can I tell another
The formula
To my equation if I have no variables?

How can I interpret one more
If I don't know
Myself?

Cold world alone

My family and friends are away
Even if try it seems like they won't stay
My boyfriend has flown
I am in a cold world alone

Where can I turn
Where no one shows concern
Their actions have shown
I am in a cold world alone

The cold wind hit my face
It seems like my eyes are filled with mace
I feel like I've been hit with a stone
I am in a cold world alone

I walk in darkness hoping to see light
Wondering if things will ever get right
I can not return home
In this world I feel so alone

I cough because I have a chill
No one cares how I feel
Everybody has grown
I am in a cold world alone

My heart is broken
Actions and words have been spoken
My music has no tone
I am in a cold world alone

My head is a puzzle
Over my body my loved ones put a muzzle
I feel as if I've been stripped to the bone
I am in a cold world alone

Life

Wanting to be accepted
But always rejected from your love
When I find myself going straight
For some reason I look back because
I love you
And it is so hard
For me to let you go
But if I stay then I know a broken heart
I will have to face

Hw many tears can I cry
For you to love me
Remember love is a two way street
and not an obligation

When I look at myself
I see the devil
Because I harvest so much hate
And I try my hardest to not be like him
But I find myself having some of his ways

It's like I am
Dead but alive
Because on earth I feel so alone
And I find myself
Looking for love
Because my heart is hurt
Some say I try too hard
To be accepted
But I'm rejected from your love

I will hate for me
To die
Knowing I haven't told you
I love you
And meant it

For a long time
How many prayers can I pray
How much longer can
I pretend
How many times
Can I watch the same rerun
It's time to change the channel
For you and me

Mankind

How can one feel so much pain
Have so much hate for mankind
I have no words to say
I have no way to succeed
I have no way to live for eternity
Knowing I will go to hell for having this feeling

How can I
Love a God
And can't love mankind unconditionally
So much pain I have
So many tears I cried
For feeling this way
I try to be strong
But the love I have
Want to hold on
To the misery
To the depression
To the sleepless nights
To the watery eyes

I don't think I will ever say thank you
For your love
I hate to look in the mirror
Because I see a face
That's filled with hate
I hear a voice
That's filled with fear

It seems like you are my demon in life
that's why my blessings don't come right
That's why my life is so hard
Because I fight back with hate
Making it hard for me to
Love

How can I love a God
How can I go to heaven
If I can't love mankind

Pain

My heart feels so much pain
Causing my eyes to pour like rain
In this miserable world my mind
Is going insane
Eve committed the biggest mistake
Now every mother will cry
Because every child will die
I was born into pain
when my mother had me she was in tears
Raising an wedlock baby
Is not as easy as it appears

I wonder does anybody die in peace
Death many people fear
But the pain we cause allows death near
We don't know our last steps
Our last words
Our last fight
So brothers and sisters let's live life right
Causing pain seems to take us down the sinning lane
Let's not die in shame
Let's not die pain

Life
Transformation

The eternal God is thy refuge, and underneath are the everlasting arms.
Deuteronomy 33-27- KJV

Life: Transformation

My soul was fed

When you pulled the trigger
The gun went bang
Over my heart was a sudden pain
I thought my life was done
But my book had just begun

I was in the middle of chapter three
Wondering why this had to happen to me
Knowing I had just been delivered
But on the ground my
Soul still shivered and quivered

My head was so furious
But at the same time
I was thanking the Lord for working so mysteriously
Off of me released a cell
That could not be bought off with bail

The bullet moved down to my heart
I did not want me and you to part
So I held on
But God's love is so strong
And no C.P.R
Was done

Stepping out on faith
Leaving you
Without a trace
For I can not return

Knowing my true blessings
I can't receive
With you inside of me

Change my colors

Make me as beautiful as a butterfly
Revise my soul
Change my colors
Bring me out
Lord have mercy on me

How do I come back
When I have slipped so far away
How do I love
When my heart harvests
So much hate
When I can't let go of the pain life has sent to me
When I make my sins my God

What do I say
How do I pray
When I have not prayed
A prayer in so long
When I don't even know your voice
It felt like my soul has gone to hell
Before my eyes
Could rest in peace

Where do I go
For I do not know how
To walk this journey of life alone
I need you Lord to strengthen me
For I 'am weak

Knowing I have to make the first step
Into salvation
Knowing if I step into salvation
My life will fly
I will fly away
Like the butterfly
My colors will change

Life: Transformation

I will not be the same
I will have a different name

For I give you all of me
Lord I need you
For my walk is not right
I tried to do it alone
But I do nothing but fail

Make me as beautiful as the butterfly
Revise my soul
Change my colors
Bring me out
Lord have mercy on me

I know

I know you love me
When everybody turns their back on me
When my family had enough of me
I know you will never give up on me

I know you're watching me
Even when I'm living life the worldly way
Not taking the steps you want me to take
I know you will always care
When everybody else doesn't understand

I know you will always make a way
When all doors are shut in my face
When my light just won't shine
The maze I know you will help me escape

When I walk thought the storm
Your blanket of love
I know I can count on

I know you sent your son down to die
For a sinner like me
So I can be free
I know with you
I will never die
But will live life eternally
I know

Life: Transformation

There is another path I can take

My steps have been taken
My path has been made
In my bed I have laid
My debts I have paid
Not knowing five years can make
A person change
I wish I could have seen the future
Maybe my soul would not be so dry
And less tears would have come from my eyes

I did know one wrong move
In the game of life
Could make my heart paralyzed
And my soul thirst
For water the world can't provide

I had to find out the hard way
That the word love loves no one
But I found someone
That had agape love for me
Every since I picked up the B.I.B.L.E
Well, just like Jesus rose from the dead
My soul was fed

Now I have to leave old times behind
And form a new frame of mind
Dig bad roots out of my garden
For they will keep me from getting further

This time around I choose
To go right even if there is
More battles for me to fight

Since I am saved by grace
I know
There is another path for me to take
My bed I can remake
And there are debts for me to pay

Living right

I am a saint wanting to get my life right
Trying to walk like Christ
Every night praying a prayer like dear God
Help me fight the temptation of life
Using forgivingness as an excuses for my sins
But this race don't end at Cavalry

Because Jesus lived pass Cavalry
So there is no excuses for me not to walk right
But I keep getting pulled back into sin
Making a commitment to follow Christ
Always letting myself break down into life
Every time I drift away I get pulled back by God

Letting myself battle between the devil and God
Not fully receiving Cavalry
That is why I can't fully live life
Finding it hard to learn from my mistakes
And live right
Not completely accepting Christ
For I am in love with my sins

I will not let the Devil use my love for sin
Against my walk with God
I can change because of Christ
Just for me was Cavalry
I can turn from wrong to right
And live a better life
God hold so much for me in life

Knowing I have to get out of sin
And live right
To receive all the things God
Left for me at Cavalry
In Jesus Christ

Life: Transformation

It is because of Christ
I can live another day in life
Because he paid the price on Cavalry
I can wash my hands like my sins
The holy spirit, the son, and the father God
Live in me, and allows me to live another day right

www.ingramcontent.com/pod-product-compliance
Lightning Source LLC
Chambersburg PA
CBHW032018290426
44109CB00013B/704